A MichKa Art Play Book Series to explore creative spirit within

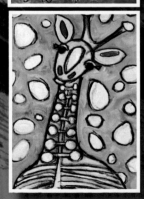

Drawing *and* Painting *with*
Michelle Miller
& Kate Carson

BOOK ONE
FUNKY ANIMALS

'Freedom
requires no trail of
breadcrumbs.'

~ M. Miller

Agio
PUBLISHING HOUSE

Other stuff by MichKa Art Play
www.MichKaArtPlay.com

EUROPEAN AND INDONESIAN ADULT WORKSHOPS

For many years, Michelle and Kate have travelled to Europe and Asia to teach drawing and painting workshops to artists of all ages who come from around the globe. We draw, we paint, we take local sojourns, we eat well and live in comfortable accommodations. Come join us in a relaxed environment while learning more about your own personal relationship with art. Find out about our next travel dates and locations at www.ArtSchoolVictoria.com. You can also contact us personally: art@michelle-miller.com

THE QUIET TEACHER FLASHCARDS

These cards are a set of 21 problem-solving flashcards for the experienced and beginner artist. When you are at *that* point in your creative process where you need a little help, you randomly draw one of the flashcards. The suggestions and examples you'll see will offer a new approach and help you move forward again. Order at MichKaArtPlay.com

Agio
PUBLISHING HOUSE
151 Howe Street,
Victoria BC Canada V8V 4K5
www.agiopublishing.com

MichKa Art Play
Book One—Funky Animals
ISBN 978-1-927755-06-8 (trade paperback)
ISBN 978-1-927755-07-5 (pdf ebook)

Cataloguing information available from Library and Archives Canada.
Printed on acid-free paper.
Agio Publishing House is a socially responsible company, measuring success on a triple-bottom-line basis.
10 9 8 7 6 5 4 3 2 1 ib

Acknowledgments

We had a great deal of help to make this project a reality and would like to say a big thank you to the following people:

Marsha and Bruce Batchelor at Agio Publishing House – we would be completely lost without you! Your input and creative ideas helped us immensely. Marsha, the graphic layout is incredible and we are so fortunate to be able to work with you. Bruce, thanks for your valuable wisdom on the publishing industry.

Jen Steele, photographer/videographer extra-ordinaire! Your kind and gentle patience never went unnoticed.

Kickstarter, for being the number one crowd-funding platform in the world for the arts – where we showcased MichKa Art Play and succeeded with our fundraising goal within two weeks.

Chris Tougas, for all your technical help and humour.

Robin Kirkpatrick, for making us accountable for the work on a weekly basis and for all of your business advice.

Our families and friends, for ongoing support on so many levels.

Café Brio, for allowing us to stage our annual children's art auction for 13 years. Showcasing the kids' art really brought significant creative voice to the kids and demonstrated the need for art within everyone's world, starting at a young age.

A very, very special thank you to all of our students who have made this project happen and taught us SO much.

~ Michelle & Kate

Why do we want to nuture creativity throughout our lives?

We believe the following ideas are just a few of the amazing benefits of having a creative mind… we're sure you can come up with more of your own!

- Creativity builds confidence which equals self-esteem and happiness

- Creative thinkers are problem solvers which in turn equals innovative thinkers

- Creativity is a non-verbal self-expression that crosses cultural borders

- Creativity fills the soul with joy and possibilities

- Lifelong art skills carry over into all other areas of one's life, such as maths and sciences and human relationships

- Creating art opens the door to your heart and imagination

'Personality is everything in art and poetry.'

Tip

the 3 E's of Play

Explore
Experiment
and
Express

"It takes a long time to paint like a child."
~ Picasso

In Michelle's Words

I've never wanted to do anything else in my life other than create art. Absolutely nothing makes me happier or makes me feel more complete.

As a child, I was unbearably shy. In fact, my best friend's brother called me *Old Boring* because I was afraid to speak or look at anyone and I'm certain I truly was boring to him at that time. But in my art, even at a young age, I felt confident. I gained more confidence as the years went by and I was constantly doing more and different kinds of art – from drawing/painting, to sculpture, weaving, photography and mixed media.

I have wonderful memories of oil painting with my mom at the kitchen table and of art classes as a teenager at school with an excellent and qualified artist/instructor, Waine Ryzak. Waine opened my eyes to so much more than painting and drawing which at the time were my only world of art. I entered university and completed two degrees in art. I never would have envisioned myself being able to teach, but when I happened upon it by chance, I found I not only liked it but was extremely adept at it too.

It started in 1996 when I was picking up my 9-year-old friend from school once a week to help her single mom out. We would go to the studio in my house to paint and draw. Each week she brought more friends until finally she just said – 'Michelle, why don't you just teach art for real?'

My passion and enthusiasm for sharing and inspiring what I have learned over the many years as an artist is fuelled by the desire to help people become who they are. Being creative makes me feel beautiful, intelligent and connected to something bigger than me. It is like a lover I cannot get enough of.

I hope to show others how to find their creative hearts and voices, and leave their own *Old Boring* behind.

~ Michelle Miller,
2014

In Kate's Words

Art is my life. Drawing, painting and creating is PURE JOY to me.

I am passionate about teaching art to children. I love their art. It's expressive and free; teaching children inspires me. I want to draw and paint like them! I want to connect with that freedom they have.

If you watch a child draw or paint, they don't care if the drawing is a little wonky, they don't care if they go over the lines, they don't care what colours they put down. And because of this, their drawings and paintings have so much energy and life!

Drawing, I have to admit, is my first love – it brings me so much joy to know that I can draw anything using the ABC's of drawing. That's why I encourage everyone and anyone to learn to draw. It's very simple. It will enhance your art and increase life's possibilities ten fold.

The goal for me is to INSPIRE everyone to play and create. Thus, this book series! So let's go CREATE together!

~ Kate Carson,
2014

Testimonials

'Alison has always expressed herself through art. Taking these art classes has exposed her to new ideas, styles and techniques which she has enthusiastically incorporated into the work she does outside of the studio. With this increased vocabulary for self-expression has come more self-confidence; it has taught her new ways of expressing herself.'

~ Carolyn Hissen, mother of Alison Hissen, age 11

'The classes have a creative impact on Owen and he will often sit and draw for a long period of time. The past spring, his school class visited the art gallery and his teacher commented on how much he knew about technique and styles... so he obviously listens!!

~ Glenn Barlow, father of Owen Barlow, age 7

'Napier loves his art classes and it has been very valuable in developing his self-confidence. Playing with colour and new techniques in painting and drawing have been key in this development.'

~ Jody Levins, mother of Napier Levins, age 6

'The art lessons have been VERY valuable to Amelie! Amelie loves to come to her art classes. Her work is wonderful! She's developed a real attachment to Kate. She is confident in regard to her art and life.'

~ Adam Bate, father of Amelie Bate, age 6

'Avery has really grown as an artist and a person while taking these art classes. Over the past 2 years she has become so confident in her artistic and creative abilities and it seems to overflow into everyday life as well. We are constantly impressed with her uses of colour and blending and her creations are something she always takes a lot of pride in.

'We have been so happy with the classes. Not only the techniques taught but because it is all done in an environment that encourages individuality and the creative process.'

~ Kerry Vaughan, mother of Avery Vaughan, age 8

Contents

FUNKY ANIMALS PROJECTS

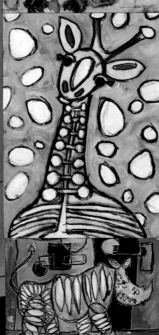

Tip: How learning to DRAW is similar to learning to READ and WRITE.

Reading and WRITing
alphabet = 26 letters
Y e t a v e m p
l o c s r

letters together = WORDS
to yes   love creativity
map

WORDS together = sentences
map to creativity

DRAWing
alphabet = 3 lines

closed lines = shapes

shapes together = image

Introduction

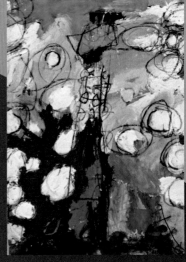

We truly believe that creative thinkers will inherit the Earth because creativity promotes spontaneity and innovation.

Some of the greatest gifts from human kind come from being creative and we want to share that gift with you and your child. We want to help you to become lifelong creative souls so that life continues to be rich and rewarding on many levels.

We love kids art and we love teaching art to kids. We love the positive effects art has on the kids and ourselves in the process. Making art creates a positive and confident individual and atmosphere. This is something we all want and need at all ages.

> 'All children make amazing art. Picasso has often confessed that he borrowed freely from the creations of children and always had their artwork hanging in his studios."
>
> ~ Robert Burridge, contemporary artist

We also believe adults will love our MichKa Art Play book series. Everyone is creative but sometimes we forget or deny our own creativity. If you would like to try something new just for fun, then these books are for you.

Every project is unique, creative and playful – NOT your typical 'how to draw and paint' book. So here is a chance for everyone to learn to play and have fun like they are 6 years old again while simultaneously learning how to draw and paint!

BE your own creative revolution because
CREATIVE THINKERS WILL INHERIT THE EARTH!

~ Michelle and Kate

This book is for all of us young and old who are kids at heart wanting to explore the creative spirit within.

Wichita ArtPlay

Here's How the Projects Work

Being creative allows each of us to simply express and be ourselves. When we produce a beautiful work of art, our confidence in ourselves grows, and grows, and grows.

Each project takes approximately 1 to 1.5 hours to complete. The projects have step-by-step guided instructions with samples of art to follow along. These instructions will take you from a blank white surface to a beautifully layered and interesting painting that is gallery worthy. Techniques are reinforced in each lesson. In some cases, there are suggestions on how you can add other elements and media to the project.

You'll find a full materials supply list on page 8 and more detail at the beginning of each project. Feel free to use whatever suits your creative inspirations.

To help each artist connect with their subject, we have also shared some fun facts. So not only will you be able to show your talents as an artist when you have completed the projects, but you will also sound like a genius!

VARIATIONS AND SUGGESTIONS

These projects encourage individual interpretation. We show you basic ways to draw and paint, then sometimes give suggestions on different compositions using a variety of media. Of course the different media variations can be used on any project. Add as many of your own ideas too because that's what art is all about. The *Variations and Suggestions* section can be found on page 49.

Before you get started on the projects, let's go through a few of the basics.

The Elements of Art

Line, Colour, Shape, Texture, Value

LINE

Just like the alphabet has 26 letters, there are really only 3 different kinds of line. We refer to this as the *ABC's of Line*.

   A. The straight line

   B. The curved line

   C. The angled line

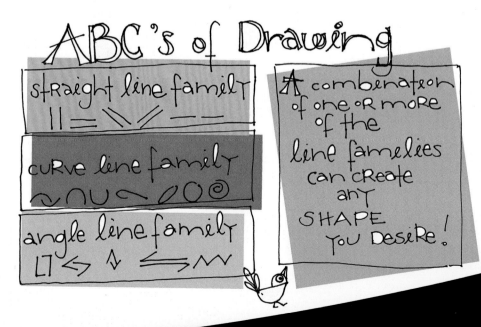

ABC's of Drawing

straight line family
|| = \\ \/ — –

curve line family
~ ∩∪ ~ ⊘○◎

angle line family
⊓ ⇦ ⋀ ⇐ ⋀⋀

A combenateon of one oR moRe of the line famelies can cReate any SHAPE you DesiRe!

Colour Wheel

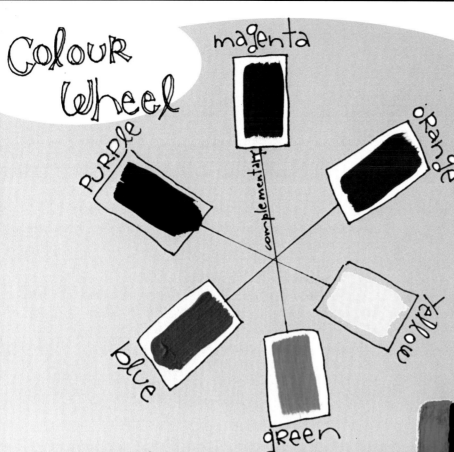

On the colour wheel you can find the opposite (complement) of a colour by drawing a straight line across. COMPLEMENTARY COLOURS are: red/green, Blue/orange, purple/yellow.

complementary colours

warm colours

cool colours

pRimary colours
RED (magenta), Yellow and blue
secondary colours
orange, green and puRple
complementary colours
colours opposite to each other on
colour wheel.

COLOUR

PRIMARY COLOURS are red, yellow, blue. These are the basic colours that you cannot mix from other colours.

SECONDARY COLOURS are orange, green and purple. These are the colours you create when you mix two of the primary colours together. Note that if you start with different versions of the primaries (ie: Cadmium red vs magenta), you will achieve different versions of secondaries. The example below uses two different yellow options.

Yellow oRche + ceRulean =

CaD. Yellow meD. + ceRulean =

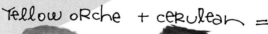

SHAPE

To draw a shape, you start with a line. When that line travels around to meet itself where it started and becomes closed, *VOILA!* you have a shape!

bumpy and busy

TEXTURE

Texture can be real or fake. By this we mean that a painting could have real texture with real bumps or scratches in it. You can also create fake texture by painting the look of those bumps or scratches. Smooth is also a type of texture.

smooth and calm

VALUE

This is usually the trickiest of the elements to remember. Value is the variation of light and dark within a colour. You can make colours lighter by mixing in various amounts of white. Make them darker by adding a bit of black. But more interesting than adding black to make them darker, add a wee bit of the opposite colour. To make reds seem lighter adding white makes pink but adding yellow makes orange.

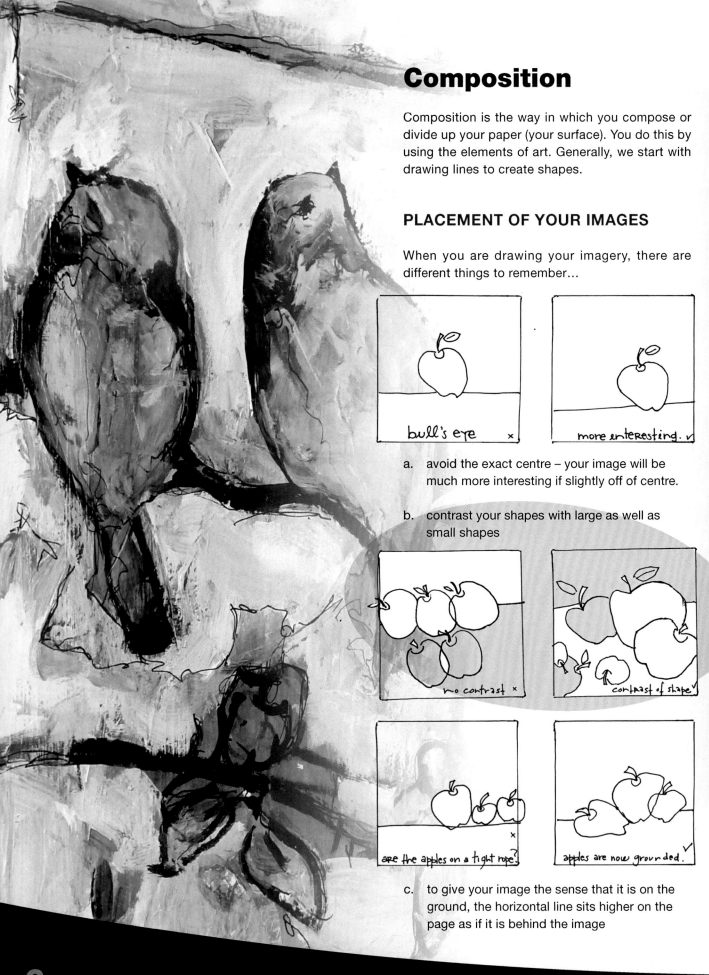

Composition

Composition is the way in which you compose or divide up your paper (your surface). You do this by using the elements of art. Generally, we start with drawing lines to create shapes.

PLACEMENT OF YOUR IMAGES

When you are drawing your imagery, there are different things to remember...

bull's eye   x   more enteresting. v

a. avoid the exact centre – your image will be much more interesting if slightly off of centre.

b. contrast your shapes with large as well as small shapes

no contrast x   contrast of shape v

are the apples on a tight rope?   apples are now grounded. v

c. to give your image the sense that it is on the ground, the horizontal line sits higher on the page as if it is behind the image

too small ✗

fill the page ✓

d. fill the page with your image and break the edge of the paper, by taking your lines right off the edges

e. vary the direction of your images – even varying the direction of the apple stem gives the painting more excitement

apples are all lined up ✗

vary direction - gives more interest. ✓

✗

overlapping gives depth. ✓

f. overlapping images gives drawings more interest and depth.

CONTRAST
IS VERY IMPORTANT

We cannot stress this enough. Often when people are working on their paintings or drawings, they have problems understanding why the art is not 'working'. A simple checklist of opposites in the elements of art is usually all it takes to know how to fix the problem.

a. **Contrast of line** – thick and thin, curvy and straight

b. **Contrast of shape** – large and small, angled and rounded

c. **Contrast of texture** – smooth and bumpy, lots of scratches and no scratches

d. **Contrast of value** – lighter blues and darker blues for example

Scratching into wet paint creates texture, breaks the edge and creates thick and thin lines

This painting is strong on value: white, grey and black

BREAKING THE EDGE
Be sure to take some of your lines right off the edge of the surface. The lines will operate like little roads leading you to enter and exit the composition.

REPETITION
Repeating a shape even if in different sizes helps to bring the composition together. It's like a hop-scotch. Your eyes know to travel around the surface of the art because it can connect the similar shapes.

Notice the texture in this painting and the use of larger and small similar shspes

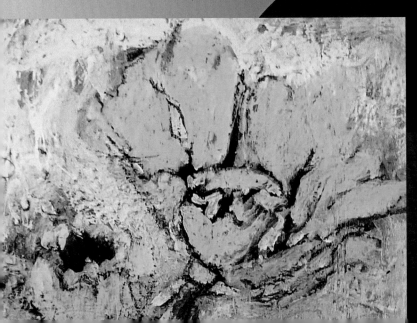

Materials

We recommend good quality supplies. It really does make a HUGE difference.

Acrylic paint colours we used for this book's Funky Animal projects:

Cadmium red   Cerulean blue
Magenta   Ultramarine blue
Cadmium yellow   Unbleached titanium
Yellow ochre   Titanium white
Pthalo green

We have kits that can be ordered that use Demco Brands paints. Contact us at art.supplies@islandblue.com.

Another choice for good kids' quality acrylic paints is Chromochryl.

For more professional acrylic paints: Golden or Stevenson's.

BRUSHES
We use two types of brushes:
Flat bristles – 3/4 inch and 1/4 inch
Round bristles – very small round for details.

SHARPIE AND CHINA MARKER (GREASE PENCIL)
We don't use erasers. If you don't like a line, you just re-draw the line. The paint covers the lines you don't want to keep. Extra lines add more energy and interest!

SOFT PASTELS
Prang makes some soft pastels known as pastellos. They are harder than your usual soft pastels so don't create as much dust. For a more punchy effect, although more expensive, Prismacolor-Nu Pastels are beautiful. You can usually buy them in a box or individually.

OIL PASTELS
We like to use oil pastels as a resist to the paints. They are also great for solid colour coverage in your art.

FIXATIVE
A fixative is just that – it fixes the pastel so it doesn't smudge. It is only needed for soft pastel or soft drawing materials. SpectraFix is a non-toxic eco-friendly fixative that is non-yellowing. For a less expensive alternative, odorless aerosol hairspray can work but may yellow over time. Be sure the room is well ventilated before using the aerosol sprays.

PAPER
We suggest Stonehenge paper. It is an archival cotton rag paper that is available in most art stores. It generally comes in sheets of 22 x 30 inches. Fold, crease and rip to get lovely deckle edges and 4 smaller sheets. The paper rips very easily on the fold. We have found Stonehenge to be a very durable paper for multimedia.

INDIA INK
We like the Speedball Super Black India Ink. It has an emollient in it (like a glue) so it is permanent.

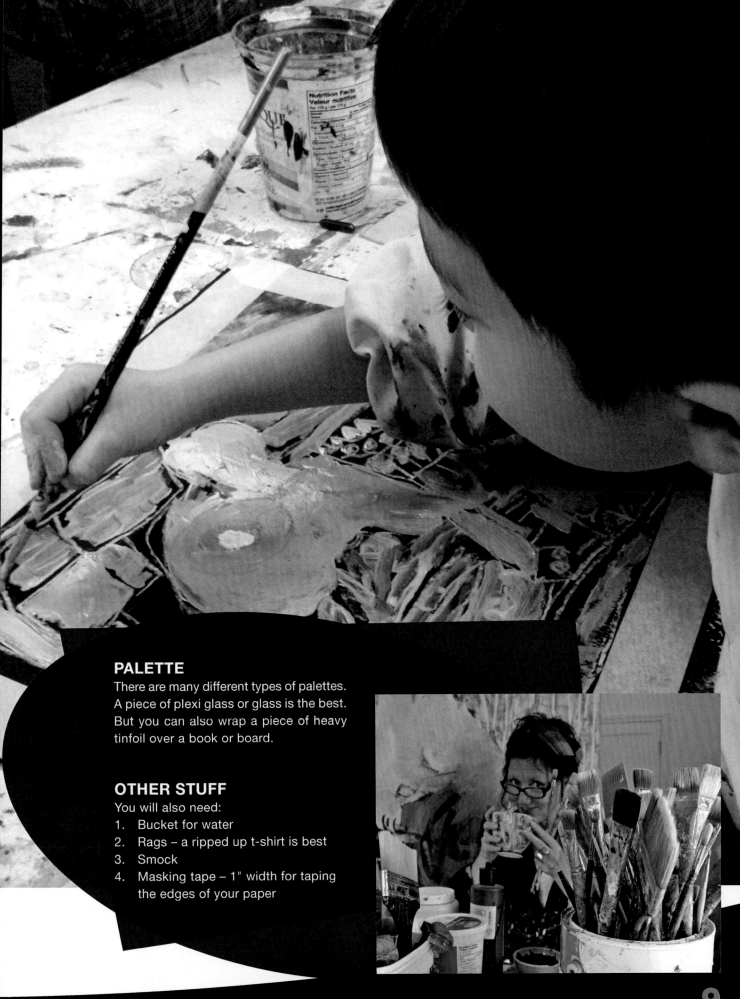

PALETTE

There are many different types of palettes. A piece of plexi glass or glass is the best. But you can also wrap a piece of heavy tinfoil over a book or board.

OTHER STUFF

You will also need:
1. Bucket for water
2. Rags – a ripped up t-shirt is best
3. Smock
4. Masking tape – 1" width for taping the edges of your paper

WALKING OWL

Owls are beautiful large birds that are active at night (nocturnal). Although we think of owls swooping down at Hallowe'en and during other mystical times, we bring our owl to life in the painting by imagining it walking rather than flying. We've all seen other birds walk across the road or field, but do owls walk? WHOOOOOOOO knows? They have a very mysterious life! YOU are the artist and it is up to you to invent a life for the owl in your painting.

SUPPLIES

- tape
- paper
- brushes
- paint
- palette
- rag
- water bucket

- sharpie
- soft pastels
- hair dryer
- hair spray or fixative
- China marker
- black India ink

Paint colours we used:
- magenta
- white
- cerulean blue
- yellow

Did you know that...

1. Owls have 3 eyelids: one for blinking, one for sleeping and one for keeping the eye clean and healthy.
2. A group of owls is called a *parliament*... this refers to wisdom and study.
3. Owls are unable to move their eyes very much within their sockets so they must turn their entire head to see in different directions... about 270 degrees.
4. Owls are very mystical animals and are often used in books and movies to portray a wise creature. Part of the owl's mystique is because it can fly silently. Owls are large birds and their wings are specially designed so that they do not create sound. Sound is created with most birds in flying when turbulence (air movement) gushes over their wings. Because owls are silent in their flying, it makes them very good at hunting. *(from animalfact.com)*

Drawing Your Walking Owl

Tape the edges of the paper. When you are done and take the tape off – *TAH DAH!* – you have a nice clean white border that frames the work.

1 The Basic Body Shape

a. With a sharpie, start by marking your basic shapes with a few guiding dots. Three dots at the top as if points of a triangle pointing down. Near the bottom of paper, do 3 more dots like the points of a triangle pointing up. ONE DOT in the middle on the left.

b. Join the dots at the top to create a 'V' shape using slightly curved lines. At the bottom, do the same with slightly curvy lines and it will create an upside-down 'V' shape.

c. On the right side, connect the top and bottom lines with a curved line bending slightly inward. On the left side, connect with 2 lines that curve slightly outward and meet in the centre dot.

2 The Beak and Forehead

a. The beak – below in the centre where the dot is in the first 'V' shape, draw a small 'V' which will be the beak. The 'V' shape is from the angle line family.

b. Above that, draw from the dots of both sides at top making two slightly curved lines downward that meet in the middle.

c. Again from the two points on top, draw an outward curving line that joins the dots.

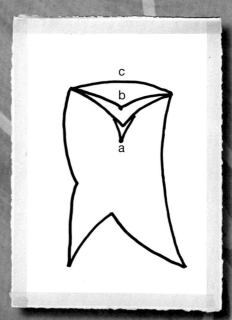

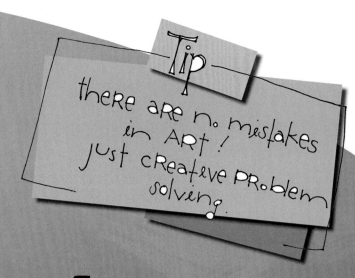

Tip

there are no mistakes
in Art!
just creative problem
solving.

3 Eyes and Ear Tufts

a. The eyes – draw two circles on either side of the beak toward the outside of the owl shape. Then, draw another smaller circle inside each of the first circle. You can set the second circle a bit higher or off side so that the owl seems to be looking in a direction.

b. For the ear tufts, the basic shapes are almost like leaves. Because owls often have one bigger than the other, we can draw them like that if we want.

   Start by drawing a curved line from the outer points of the head. Draw an opposite curved line so that it meets at the top of the first one. Repeat this smaller on the inside of this 'leaf' shape.

4 The Wings

a. Starting at the point of the head below the left ear tuft, draw a large curved line almost to the bottom of that leg. 'Jump' over the left leg with your sharpie and continue to give depth by making the wing seem behind the leg. Create a zig-zag with straight lines (angle line family) and finish at the leg.

b. For the right wing, draw a curved line from the right point of the head below the ear to the outer edges of your paper. Then, draw a zig-zag line again using straight lines and finish it at the side of the right leg.

5 The Feet

We are going to stylize the feet for the owl in this drawing. To stylize means to exaggerate or make a design that refers to the actual thing you are drawing. This is very common in art-making. It is also a lot of fun!! Feel free to add your own stylized additions to the owl and any drawing!!

Owls have 4 toes. In reality, they have 3 toes facing forward and one back. This is quite common in many birds.

a. On each of the tips of the legs start by drawing 4 small shapes. Each shape is like a leaf, just like the ear tufts and are made up of 2 curved lines facing each other and joining at a point on either end.

b. For the 'toe nails' or talons, draw a little circle at the point of each leaf-shaped toe.

c. Now you are done drawing the basic shape of the owl. It's time to make up a story about your owl and draw details to go with (illustrate) the story. Does it wear glasses? Walk on a branch?

6 Background and Decorated Positive and Negative Space

On the owl... (the positive space)

This part is completely up to you in how you want to decorate your owl. We have added stripes and circles and the suggestion of eye lashes.

In the back ground... (the negative space)

To make it seem as though the owl is walking on a branch, draw a curvy line from one edge of the paper to the other but jump over the feet with your sharpie. This will make it seem like the feet are in front and on the line. To make the line look like a branch, draw another curvy line beside the first one. Add leaves by drawing two curved lines facing each other and meeting at points at the top and bottom. Draw a curved line through the middle of these shapes to show the vein of the leaf.

To add interest to the background (remember the negative space is just as important as the positive space), we decided to draw the suggestion of a full moon in the right top behind the owl. Owls are nocturnal (active at night) so the moon demonstrates this.

To give contrast to all the curved lines, we added some straight lines in the negative space. Take the lines to the edge of the paper (break the edge!) so that you use the entire paper.

Painting Your Owl

'Once in a blue moon you will see an owl walking…' could be the title of this painting.

- magenta
- white
- cerulean blue
- yellow

7 Underpainting

Remember that the underpaint ('underpants' as we like to call it) is just the first layer to go under the rest of your colours. It gives the other colours complexity and interest.

a. We used magenta for this project's underpaint.

b. Using your big brush with lots of water on it but not too much paint, spread your colour all over your paper from edge to edge. Wipe it with a rag if there is a bit too much paint. This will allow you to see clearly the sharpie line drawing.

c. Dry very well with a hair dryer.

8 Adding White

Remember that white is the colour we look at first. White is technically not a colour but a tint. Black is not a colour either, but a shade. But for here, we will refer to them as colours as they come out of the tube and it simplifies explanation.

a. Using a clean, smaller brush (no water on the brush), add some white to areas so that it is evenly placed in your painting. Remember to do this in the negative space and the positive space (clean your brushes in the water as you paint, dabbing off any excess on a rag to dry). Just because a spot is painted white does not mean it has to remain white. Later, you can paint over the white, leaving just a bit of an edge of the white showing.

c. Dry with a hair dryer.

9 Mixing Colours

a. For the moon, we mixed blue with a bit of white to create a light blue which makes the moon seem like it is glowing.

b. Using the magenta that we still had left on our palette and a bit of white mixed in, we painted the eyes and part of the ear tufts. For the rest of the owl, we painted it yellow.

10 Night-time Background

a. To make it seem like night-time, mix the blue with magenta to create a purple and paint all of the background except the moon. You can also lighten the purple by mixing a bit of white into it. Having the magenta and white underneath will make the background come alive!

b. Once we had the purple completed, we felt as though the yellow parts of the owl needed some 'punching up'. So we mixed a bit of white with yellow on our palette and re-painted the yellow areas. Notice how much it now 'pops' out! We also painted the branch and leaves.

   If you are wanting to create a green in the leaves, mix the blue and yellow together ...*VOILA!!!* GREEN.

11 Re-inking the Lines

When the paint is dry, use India ink with a very small brush and hold it straight up and down for very fine lines. Paint ink over the original drawn lines of as much of the work as you like. If you have big blobs of ink, keep your painting flat. Use a paper towel to gently blot the blobs so that they don't run. Now is the time to be sure to **dry very well** with the hair dryer.

12 Finishing with Pastel

a. Once your painting is completely and totally dry, draw beside most of the black lines using the white soft pastel. If you want to use other pastels to add more colour, by all means go ahead and have fun!!!

b. Spray with fixative, in a ventilated area, to stabilize the pastel and then let dry.

c. Remember to take the tape off so you'll have a clean crisp border. Your painting is done! It is ready for signing in the lower right corner above the tape.

WHIRLY BIRDS

We've all seen birds in the garden fly quickly past our eyes and dance around the flowers. They seem to whirl around nature! Their playground is the garden and they make their fun flights of play a delight to watch. With this in mind, we designed the Whirly Bird project with pom-pom flowers as their amusement park.

SUPPLIES

- masking tape
- paper
- brushes
- paint
- palette
- rag
- water bucket
- sharpie
- soft pastels
- hair dryer

Paint colours we used:
- titanium white
- magenta
- cerulean blue
- pthalo green
- cadmium yellow medium

Did you know that...

1. Birds have hollow bones which makes them lighter for flying.
2. Some birds are intelligent enough to create and use tools.
3. Hummingbirds can fly backwards.
4. There are nearly 10,000 different species of birds.
5. Scientists believe that birds evolved from dinosaurs. *(from animalfact.com)*

Drawing Your Whirly Bird

Tape the edges of the paper so that you will have a nice clean edge on the paper when you remove it from the final art.

1 Basic Shape of the Body and Head

a. The head – draw a curved line that looks like an upside down 'U' or small upside down half-circle.

b. The body – draw a straight line from left side of the end point of the head and continue the straight line for the top of the body.
    Draw a curved line like a large half circle for the belly connecting the two ends of the straight line. Give the bird a big belly like he's just eaten a lot of worms!

2 Beak and Eyes

a. The beak – draw 2 angled lines from the head that meet at a point forming a sideways 'V'. Then, draw a straight line on the inside of that 'V' from the point to the head so that it splits the 'V'.

b. The eye – draw a small circle on the head opposite the beak and fill in that circle to form a dot.
    Draw a bigger circle around the dot.

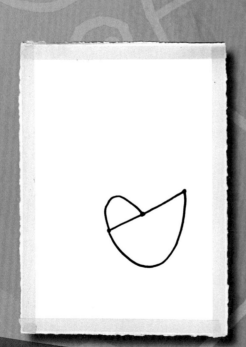

3 Legs and Tail

a. The legs – at the bottom of the belly, use angle lines to make a 'V' for one leg and repeat for second leg.

b. The tail – use curved lines to create 3 oval shapes on the end of the body point with the largest oval shape in the middle. The oval shapes are like loops. There can be more and can be made long if you like.

DRAWING THE BASIC SHAPES
The basic shapes are the outlines that hold all the details and visual information of the animal you are drawing.

4 Pom-pom Flowers

a. The ground – to ground your whirly bird on a large flower, draw a curved line from the bottom of the paper near the middle, to the right side of the paper above the corner. Be sure that the curved line touches the feet of the whirly bird.

b. The pom-pom flowers – draw 5 circles (not perfectly round) around the whirly bird but draw them in small, medium and large sizes. The different sizes are important in your composition to show contrast. Contrast is important for interest and for creating depth.

c. Inside each circle, but not directly in the middle, draw a smaller circle.

d. The stems – start at the centre circle and draw slightly curved lines side by side down to the ground. To make it look as though the flowers are behind the whirly bird, when you are drawing the curvy stems, jump over the bird and continue below on the other side which makes some shapes seem like they are in front of other shapes. This creates more depth.

5 Design Your Bird and the Background

Add design of your choice to the pom-pom flowers and bird. Make it as simple or fancy as you like! Add in lines in the background to divide up the space. Have fun!

Painting Your Bird

We kept this painting simple in colour using mainly cool colours. The contrast of the white background keeps the image fresh and calm. The orange in the tail feathers and beak is a mix of magenta and yellow.

Paint Colours

- cerulean blue
- magenta
- pthalo green
- white
- yellow

6 Underpainting

a. With your big brush wet with lots of water, dip it in a bit of the paint and cover the entire surface. Remember that when there is enough water on the brush the paint is thinned enough so you can see through to your drawing.

b. We used pthalo green for our underpaint.

7 White

a. Using pure white and your wider brush with no water, paint only the background areas in-between the lines.

b. Dry well with the hair dryer.

8 The Bird and Pom-pom Flowers

a. Mixing cerulean blue with magenta, we created a purple and painted the pom-pom flowers and centre of our bird's eye. With white and a tiny bit of cerulean blue we made a very light blue and painted the bird but left the wing more white than blue.

b. Yellow was used for the center of the flowers as well as the beak, eye and feet.

c. Inside the pattern on the tail feathers we mixed magenta and yellow to create orange. Dry well.

9 Adding Finger Touches

Sometimes we just want to get into the paint with our fingers and touch up some areas with paint. So we did. But to do this, you have to be gentle and NOT finger paint all over. We dabbed a little yellow and blue in the background around the shapes. Dry with the hair dryer.

10 Ink and Soft Pastel

a. With a tiny brush, use some India ink to outline your shapes. Dry well so the ink does not smudge. Use a light coloured soft pastel to contrast the black ink by drawing lines beside the ink.

b. In a well ventilated area, spray with a fixative to stabilize the pastel. Let dry.

c. Take the tape off and sign your beautiful art!!!

Tip

a gReat Painting is
LayeReD.
LayeRing gives the
Painting moRe DePth,
eneRgy and interest!

ARISTO-COOL CAT

It is commonly believed cats were first kept as pets in ancient Egypt. Queen Cleopatra had cats and her cats probably had their own fancy beds and servants, too. Cats are lovable but do tend to have cool personalities and do things ONLY when they want. This is why we have titled our project Aristo-Cool Cat.

SUPPLIES

- masking tape
- paper
- brushes
- paint
- palette
- rag

- water bucket
- sharpie
- soft pastel
- hair dryer
- hair spray or fixative

Paint colours we used:
- white
- magenta
- red
- yellow ochre
- cerulean blue

Did you know that...

1. Most female cats are right pawed while male cats are left pawed.
2. Cats never meow at other cats, just humans.
3. Cats sleep for 70% of their lives. This means when a cat is 10 years old it has only been awake for 3 years of its life.
4. A group of cats is called a 'clowder'
5. Cats make about 100 different sounds whereas dogs make only 10.
6. Cats can drink salt water (if they have to) and their bodies can convert it into usable fresh water that their bodies need.

(from animalfact.com)

Drawing Your Aristo-Cool Cat

Tape the edges of the paper so that you will have a nice clean edge on the paper when you remove it from the final art.

1 The Head and Eyes

a.   The head – draw a horizontal oval in the upper half of the paper so there is room to draw the body below.

b.   The eyes – draw two curved lines from outside of the head to the inside. Join another curved line to each of the first, bending the other way to connect and make the basic eye.

c.   Draw a small circle in the bottom corner of each eye to form the iris.

d.   Draw a curved line above each eye joining in the corner to form the eyelids.

2 The Mouth and Ears

a.   The mouth – draw a small 'U'-shaped curved line attached to the head at the bottom.

b.   The ears – on top of the points of each eye, draw a slightly curved line going up and inward.

c.   At the top end of that curved line, draw another downward curved line to the head.

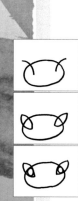

As you begin to draw, think of how there might be a story in your painting. Make up a story. Ask questions. Make up answers. A story in a painting is called a narrative. Once you start to develop your narrative, you can add extra drawings and detail into your art to match your story. It is great fun to use your imagination in this way!

3 The Face Fur, Nose and Whiskers

a. The face fur – on either side of the face using angle lines, draw zig-zag lines that have 3 points. You could make them longer and droopy too.

b. Between the eyes, draw an inward curved line from the top of the head so that a bent 'V' shape is formed with the point near the middle of the head.

c. The nose is a little heart shape with two little straight lines to the bottom of the oval shape.

d. The whiskers – draw slightly curved lines from both sides of the nose area.

4 The Body

a. Starting on either side of the mouth, draw a slightly outward curving line for the neck area continuing to widen and then curve inward and downward. Repeat on the other side.

b. From the end of each of those lines draw short straight lines that angle slightly up.

c. Join those short lines with a curved upside-down 'U' shape.

Did you know that it is natural for people to look at the whites or the lightest parts of a painting first? If you have very light colours evenly placed in your composition, the eye will look all around the painting. You WANT people to look at the entire painting and not just parts of it.

6 Background Box

Angle line family – A rectangle is made up of straight lines. When drawing a rectangle to make it seem like it is behind the cat, you need to draw the lines and then jump over the cat and continue those lines on the other side.

The box is important in this composition because it creates an anchor to the background space for the cat. It gives the sense of having a large space for the cat to sit in and it frames the cat making him important in the picture!

5 The Feet and Tail

a. The feet – using straight lines, draw small outward angled rectangles (angle line family) at the bottom of each leg.

b. Using curved lines, draw three upside-down 'U's in a row for the toes on each foot.

c. Draw a straight line across the bottom of the toes to 'close' the 'U' shapes. Draw short straight lines in each of the 'U's for the claws so that they hang outside of the feet.

d. The tail – from the outward curve below the neck on the right side, draw a curving line like an 'S'. Draw the line again beside the first and join at the point of the tail.

7 Decorating Your Aristo-cool Cat!

This is where you get to decide the personality of your cat. It can have a bowtie, a funky hat, a dress, polka-dots.... YOU make it up!

Painting Your Cat

We think this cool-cat could be an artist wearing a beret and perhaps having his portrait painted, too!

Paint Colours

- white
- magenta
- yellow ochre
- crimson red

Oil or Chalk Pastels:
- cerulean blue

8 The Underpaint

a. We used magenta for the underpaint but feel free to use whatever colour you like.

b. Dry with a hair dryer before moving on to the next step.

9 White

a. Paint in some areas using white with a clean dry brush so that your paint is thicker and opaque (opaque means that you cannot see through it).

b. Be sure to paint some of both the positive and negative areas (the cat and its background).

10 Painting the Cool-Cat

a. We are going to start by building the texture with some paint and then add soft pastel.

b. We used yellow ochre mixed with a bit of white for the cat and red for his fashion accessories. If the colours smudge together as it did here, this is okay. Great, even. You can keep it like that or paint over it! It's just paint!

11 Background— Pastels

a. Here we used soft pastel in cool colours (blues and greens) to contrast the warm colours of the cat.

b. Be energetic with your lines and marks. Go crazy creating!

12 Background –
White Paint
on Pastels

a. Using the white paint and not too much water on our brush, we painted over some of the pastel in the background. WATCH how the paint blends with the pastel! Very Cool-io! Leave some areas pastel, and some areas paint. This is another type of contrast in one of the elements of art – *texture*.

b. At this point, it is up to you if you want to do more and enhance the lines of the cat and background. If so, use ink or soft pastel. Be sure to spray this work with fixative when done so it doesn't smudge.

c. It's now time to remove the tape for those wonderful crisp edges!

Taking your lines over the edge of the paper onto the tape is called 'breaking the edge'. It allows your eyes to look at the line and enter or exit the picture as if the lines were roads.

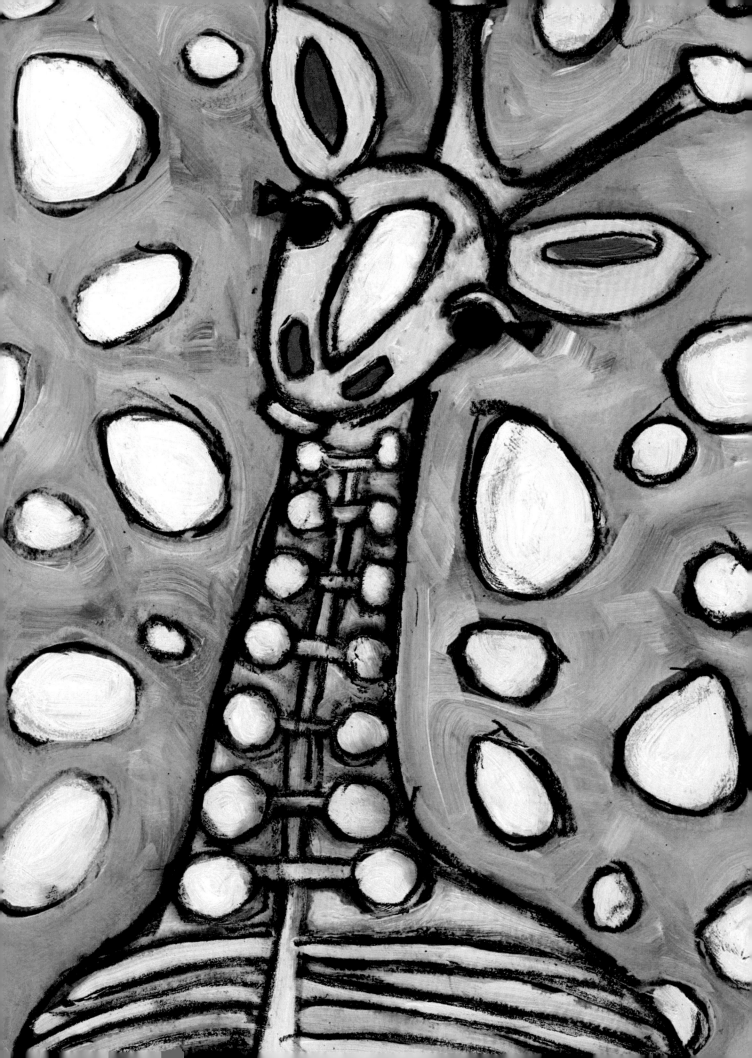

X-RAY GIRAFFE

The giraffe is a beautiful and graceful animal. In this project, we look at not just the outside of the giraffe but the inside too. It is as if the giraffe is having an x-ray taken and we see the bones in the neck. Its spots have all popped off to decorate the background.

This project is an awesome way to demonstrate what we usually think of as an 'ugly' skeleton. Any image in a painting can be 'beautiful'.

Why do we do this instead of making a perfectly traditional giraffe? Because we can! Remember that this is art. YOU are the artist! It is about your imagination. Not about reality.

SUPPLIES

- masking tape
- paper
- brushes
- paint
- palette
- rag
- water bucket
- sharpie

- India ink
- soft pastels
- China marker
- hair dryer
- hair spray or fixative

Paint colours we used:
- white
- magenta
- blue
- yellow
- orange (under paint)

Did you know that...

1. The giraffe is the tallest mammal at 5 to 6 metres (15 to 20 ft)! It can look into a second storey window without even standing on its tip toes.
2. Giraffes have the same number of vertebrae as humans but theirs are elongated.
3. They have a 50 cm (20 inch) tongue which helps to grab leaves off branches.
4. When their babies are born, they drop approximately 1.45 metres (5 ft.) to the ground. OUCH!! *(from animalfact.com)*

Drawing Your X-ray Giraffe

Tape the paper edges. These edges will be the place you will hold your painting and the tape will keep it clean.

1 Head, Mouth and Neck

a. Draw a curved line to create an egg shape about the size of your fist. This will be the head.

b. At the bottom part of the head, draw a curved line that resembles the letter 'C' so that it is attached to the head. This will be the mouth.

c. For the neck, draw a line on either side of the head. Each line will curve outward as you reach the bottom of the page to form the shoulders.

2 The Eyes

a. Giraffes have big fluttery eyes. This makes them look gentle and kind, so draw an upside-down curved line on either side of the head. Add another curved line underneath to create a rainbow shape.

b. Draw circles underneath those curves. These are the eyeballs.

c. Draw tiny triangles at the end of the curved rainbow shapes. These are the eyelashes.

3 Ears and Crown

a. The ears – giraffes have large ears that are shaped like leaves, so draw a curved line and then another curved line so that they both meet at the ends to form points like a leaf.

b. Do the same for the inside shape, but only smaller.

c. The crown – make a 'U'-shaped curved line slightly above the top of the head.

d. Draw a slightly curved line outwards on either side of the 'U' shape that attaches to the head.

e. Draw a flattened circle or oval to cap off where the 'U' and the outer lines meet to complete the crown.

4 Crest and Nostrils

a. Draw 2 small ovals in the bottom of the head shape for the nostrils.

b. For the crest, draw a triangle with slightly curved corners.

The background in art is the negative space, the space that surrounds the main object.

The main object is the giraffe which is also known as the positive space.

5 The Bones (the X-ray)

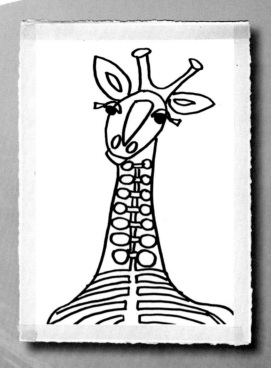

In the neck there are small bones called vertebrae. When the neck gradually joins into the chest, the rib cage takes over for the main bones.

a. On the inside of the neck, draw small circles on either side of the long neck.

b. Join these circles with two straight lines, side to side. Then, connect all of these shapes (bones) with two straight lines running down the centre of the neck.

c. For the ribs, the centre line continues downward, but it has lines right to left that are slightly curved downward towards the slope of the shoulders.

Art by Astrid, age 5

6 The Spots

a. In the background or negative space, let's draw some spots!

b. Be sure to make them different sizes. They do not all have to be round. Some could be square-ish with rounded edges. Create contrast in your sizes and shapes.

Painting The Giraffe

The colours we choose are certainly NOT the colours you must use. Using your imagination can be freeing. Remember that this is not a photograph of a giraffe and it is not about real colours. YOUR giraffe can be pink!!! It can have long lashes and a necklace. It can wear a tie and have a hat. It could also wear glasses. Add different things to match the story you are creating for it!

Paint Colours

- white
- yellow
- cerulean blue
- magenta
- use your left-over orange undercolour

7 The Undercolour

a. Orange makes a great undercolour which is what we used here. Use your large brush and lots of water to spread the underpaint over the entire painting. With more water on your brush, you can see your drawing. Wipe it with a rag if the paint is too thick.

b. Dry it with a hair dryer.

8 White

a. Start with white to paint areas of your choice. You want this paint to be thicker than the undercolour so don't use any water on your brush.

b. Paint both the negative and positive areas with some white (both the giraffe and the background).

9 Colours

Choose only a few colours and create new colours by mixing. Be sure to have white areas and pure bright areas of colour. The underpaint will show through a little bit, giving more life to your painting. The underpaint is more exciting than just white paper!

a. We started with the blue in the background around the spots.

b. Using the yellow, we mixed it with a bit of white and painted the giraffe but left the bones white.

c. With magenta and a bit of white, we mixed them together to get a lighter pink and painted inside the ears and nostrils.

d. DRY your painting completely when you are done.

10 Black and White Pastel

To ensure the painting has lots of 'pop', it's fun to finish it with the ultimate contrast of black and white (and other colours if you like).

a. Using a black soft pastel, draw your original shapes and lines over the paint.

b. With a white soft pastel, draw beside some of those black lines. Remember that the lines do not have to be exactly tight against one another. A line has its own personality and can bend a bit further away from the original lines. This is called 'offsetting'.

c. We added in a bit of magenta pastel around the bones so that the pink in the ears and nostrils would match and be more noticeable. We also added a bit of green pastel in some areas just for contrast.

d. Spray fixative and sign your art.

You have now completed your X-ray Giraffe. It's time to take the tape off and have that TAH-DAH moment!

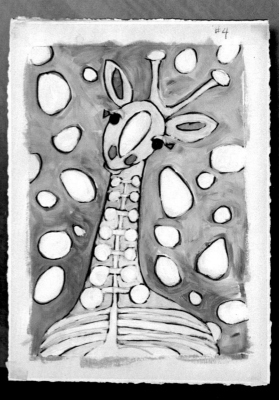

DESIGNO-RHINO

The rhinoceros is native to Africa and Southeast Asia. When we look at a rhino, we often imagine that they must be remainders of the dinosaur family. Although they are often covered in mud and their thick skin is a grey-brown colour, we chose to jazz up the rhino in designer colours and patterns.

SUPPLIES

- masking tape
- paper
- brushes
- paint
- palette
- rag

- water bucket
- sharpie
- India ink
- soft pastels
- China marker
- hair dryer

Paint colours we used:
- white
- blue
- yellow ochre
- red

Did you know that...

1. Rhinoceros run on their tippy-toes and can run up to 35 km an hour. They only have 3 toes!
2. A group of rhinos is called a 'Crash'.
3. They are critically endangered due to poaching for their horn.
4. The longest known horn was 4 feet long (as tall as the average 8 year old).
5. Rhinoceros love to roll in mud and dust to create their own sunblock.
6. They have VERY poor eyesight so they attack first and ask questions later.
(from animalfact.com)

Drawing Your Designo-Rhino

Tape the edges of the paper so that you'll have a clean border.

1 The Head

a.   The eye – close to the right side of the paper, draw a small curved line like a flat upside-down 'U'. Draw a dot underneath so it is touching the curved line. Draw a curved line like a flat 'U' underneath the dot, and an upside-down flat 'U' above for the eyebrow.

b.   The small horn and forehead – lower than the eye, draw a 'V' shape pointing toward the top right corner of your paper. This is the small horn. Add on a slightly curved line for the forehead.

c.   Larger horn – from where you left off at the end of the small horn 'V', draw a curved line upward about to the height of the eye. Then a curved line downward below the 'V' so that this last line forms a 'J'.

d.   Mouth and jaw – draw a little curved line like a 'U' and then continue with another curved line like a large extended flattened 'C' that sits on a slight angle.
     In the small 'U' shape below the large horn, draw a dot as if the rhino is whistling.

e.   The ears – on top of the forehead line, draw a smaller curved line like a smile. Draw an opposite curved line on top of the first joining the corners. This will look like a leaf. Draw a small circle inside that leaf shape.
     For the other ear, draw a wonky oval shape beside the first ear and add a smaller wonky oval inside it.

2 The Body and Tail

a. The body – from the bottom of the left ear, draw a slightly curved line going upward to a rounded point then drop downward to form a very large flattened upside down 'U' that joins back near the ear.

   On the left, add another big 'C' for the middle body section. A third 'C', slightly lower, is the rhino's hindquarters.

b. The tail – from the top of the last 'C' by the swayback, draw a curved line that bends and is pointing upward. Draw another curved line beside it. Finish with a small triangle on the end.

3 The Front and Back Legs, Feet and Toes

a. Front right leg – from the bottom of the large shoulder shape, draw with curved lines, a large oval that overlaps it.

   For the foot, draw an oval overlapping the leg oval.

b. Front left leg – just to the left of the first leg shape, draw a slightly curved line from the bottom of the body and continue it to create a large 'U' that touches the first leg.

   For the foot, draw a large oval overlapping the leg.

c. The toes – draw three small 'U's that are attached to each foot.

d. For the back legs, feet and toes, you can repeat the above steps.

When you draw with the sharpie and you are not happy with the shapes or the lines, not to worry!! The paint will cover much of it. That is why there are no mistakes in art, because you will see such beautiful unexpected things start to happen in your drawings and paintings!

4 The Ground

Having a sense of ground will attach the rhino so it doesn't seem like he is floating in space.

With a straight line that starts at one end of the paper and a bit higher than the bottom of the feet, draw across to the other side of the paper jumping over the rhino when it is in the way.

5 Decorate Your Rhino

No matter how you choose to design your rhino, its personality will begin to develop as you go along.

We chose to repeat curved but pointed shapes. As a result, the rhino looks like he is made of springs.

Painting Your Rhino

Paint Colours

- white
- yellow ochre
- red
- blue

Our rhino seemed to us to be modeling his new designer 'coat' as he walked down the fashion ramp whistling. We imagined a stage and bright colourful lights in the background.

6 The Undercolour

We used yellow ochre for this project. Using your big brush and water, spread the paint over the entire paper, and dry well.

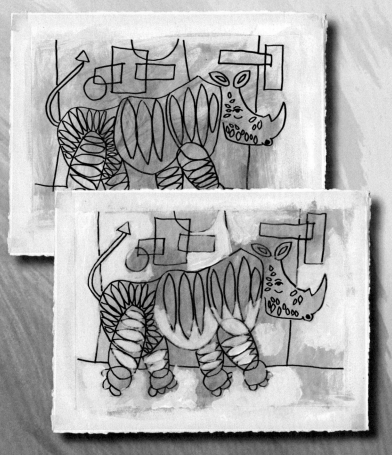

7 White

Using your big brush that has little water on it, loosely paint some areas of both the background and foreground spaces (negative and positive spaces). Leave areas of the underpaint showing.

8 Background

a. Choose your colours and paint in your background. Try to move your brush in different directions so that the brush strokes are not all the same or in one direction – remember CONTRAST! This gives a nice variation of texture and value change as the paint will blend differently on the paper than if it was all going in one direction.

b. We used cerulean blue, alizarin crimson and yellow. We mixed the blue and crimson to make purple. You can even add white to make it light purple. PLAY and MIX your colours! We added some yellow into the rhino. Yellow is a bit transparent (you can see through it).

9 More White Paint and Ink

a. We felt like the rhino needed more 'pop' so added in some white paint. We mixed the crimson with some white to enhance the pinks in the background again, and then ink and a tiny brush to go over the lines. The white and black contrast gives nice 'splash'!

b. Dry the ink *very well* so that it doesn't smudge on the painting.

10 Soft Pastel

a. Choose a couple of different pastel colours and draw beside your black ink. The extra lines can give extra exciting energy to the art! Use the ink only as a guide and find new paths for these colours.

b. As soon as everything is dry, sign your name, spray on a fixative, then take off the tape to reveal your Designo-Rhino with personality!

Whirly Bird, Aristo-Cool Cat, X-ray Giraffe, and Designo-Rhino!
VARIATIONS & SUGGESTIONS

There is an endless number of options for creating your own variations in each of these projects. Of course, using different colours is one, but also change the story and try drawing additional images and patterns into your composition.

Using different materials within your art is also an excellent option. If you don't have a lot of time or many materials, simply use and do what you can. Felt pens, water colours and oil pastels are very fun to use. The main thing is to stay creative.

For something really fun to do and perhaps with a friend, try using a large piece of paper (22 by 30 inches is a standard size for the Stonehenge paper we use). You could draw and paint more than one funky animal on the paper creating a FUNKY ANIMAL ZOO!

Here are a few variations that we played with...

Tips for a Great Composition

use strong CONTRAST in all the 5 ELEMENTS

line: thick and thin, CURVY and straight
shape: large and small, angled and Round.
COLOUR: Dark and light, cool and warm
texture: smooth and bumpy, lots of scratches and no scratches.
value: Dark and light

ask yourself 'is there CONTRAST in my.....?

1 Whirly Bird

a. Use acrylic paints for your undercolour with chalk pastels on top once the paint is dry. Notice that there are two birds here. You can add as many Whirly Birds or pom-pom flowers as you like!

b. Try drawing two Whirly Birds on one paper and have them looking in different directions. To make it look like a bird is facing in a different direction, the beak can be drawn on various sides of the head.

c. Try using lots of white chalk pastel on top of the dry acrylic paint. If you start with a dark undercolour, the white pastel can really soften the look of the painting.

d. Experiment with water colours in some areas and oil pastel in others.
   We started with red and yellow watercolour on damp paper, and then dried the paper very well.
   Then, we used blue, yellow and green oil pastels to colour in some other areas for a different texture!

2 Aristo-Cool Cat

Layering oil pastel and acrylic paints is a fun and interesting technique to explore.

a. Start with acrylic paint as your underpaint colour. When very dry, use oil pastels to colour soliidly in some areas. Put another layer of acrylic paint using white in the negative space.

b. When dry, place the sticky side of wide masking tape everywhere on top of the painting, press, then peel off. This will reveal fabulous and unexpected texture. The oil pastel works as a 'resist' against the paint, meaning the paint does not completely stick to it.

3 X-ray Giraffe

Try using water colour and coloured felt pens. Draw as usual with a s harpie.

a. Leave some areas plain white (from the paper) to show contrast. You can paint the water colour on dry paper or make your paper damp with a spray water bottle and play with the different effects.

4 Designo-Rhino

This Designo-Rhino has the designs in the negative space and the rhino is left plain. Fill the page with some of your own designs around the rhino! This gives a contrast of busy against the calm areas of the animal. This beast was painted with water colour and then outlined with white chalk pastel when the paint was dry.

Move your brush strokes in different directions. Try using more than one colour for the negative space.

After the paint is dry, use a combination of soft pastel and oil pastel for fun. Remember your contrast of light and dark!

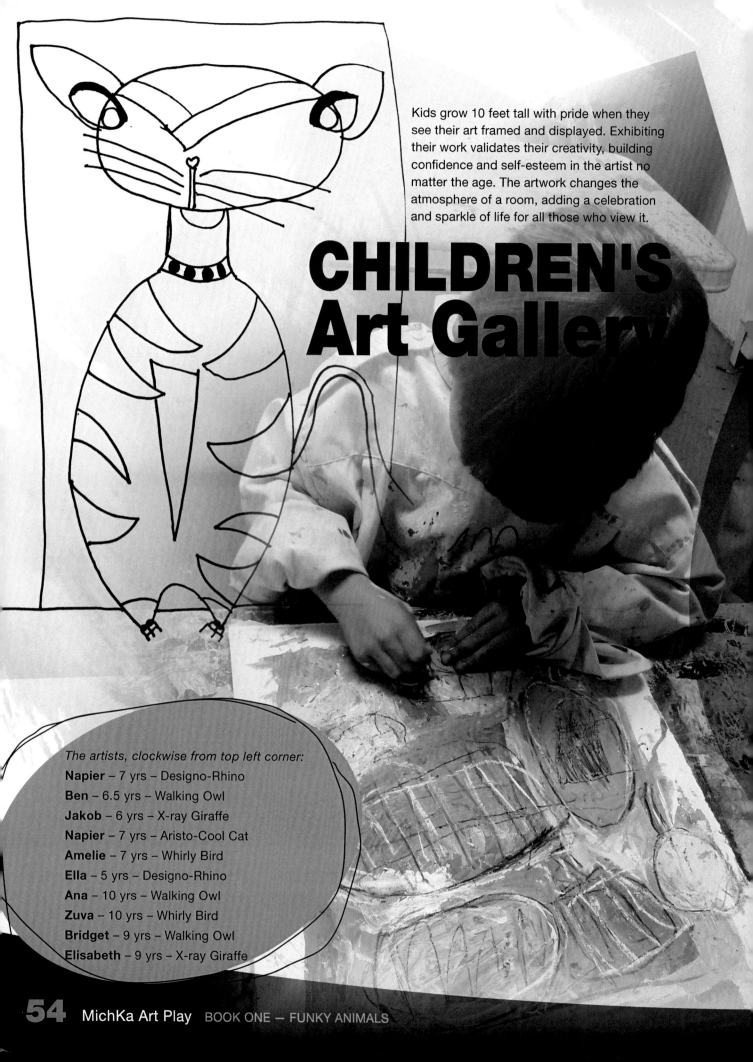

Kids grow 10 feet tall with pride when they see their art framed and displayed. Exhibiting their work validates their creativity, building confidence and self-esteem in the artist no matter the age. The artwork changes the atmosphere of a room, adding a celebration and sparkle of life for all those who view it.

CHILDREN'S Art Gallery

The artists, clockwise from top left corner:

Napier – 7 yrs – Designo-Rhino

Ben – 6.5 yrs – Walking Owl

Jakob – 6 yrs – X-ray Giraffe

Napier – 7 yrs – Aristo-Cool Cat

Amelie – 7 yrs – Whirly Bird

Ella – 5 yrs – Designo-Rhino

Ana – 10 yrs – Walking Owl

Zuva – 10 yrs – Whirly Bird

Bridget – 9 yrs – Walking Owl

Elisabeth – 9 yrs – X-ray Giraffe

'Logic will get you from A to B.
Imagination takes you everywhere.'

~ Albert Einstein

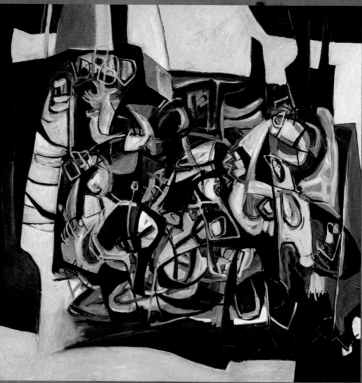

Biography

MICHELLE MILLER

B.F.A. Visual Arts
Triple Major in Painting, Drawing, & Printmaking
B.A. Art History

Born in Saskatchewan, Canada

Michelle Miller works as a full time artist from her studio in Victoria, BC, Canada where she has lived for more than 30 years. She has exhibited in Canada, United States and Asia and her work is part of private collections throughout the world. She also teaches art internationally to students of all ages, ranging from young children in Taiwan to experienced painters on foreign retreats.

'I lean toward the personal in my own artwork. I attempt to create visual poetry from life experience connecting my artistic materials with significant memories or thoughts. In essence, I am documenting my visceral history thus making it real in the here and now, not to be forgotten. By creating my art in this manner, I feel it creates for me a sense of place in the world and a connection to others.'

Left
Conversations with the Moon – 2011 – mixed media on board

Right
Past and Present – 2013 – mixed media on wood

Facing page, clockwise from top left:
Fodder – 2010 – oils on canvas
Dead Sea – 2010 – mixed media on board
Coffee and a Smoke – 2014 – mixed media on canvas
Man from U.N.C.L.E. – 2007 – oils on canvas
Sangria – 2009 – acrylics and grease pencil on paper
Tethered to the Clouds – 2010 – mixed media on canvas
Untangling the Knot – 2010 – mixed media on canvas

Biography

KATE CARSON

B. Ed.

Born in Victoria, British Columbia, Canada

Kate Carson is a self-taught artist. Although a school teacher by trade, it was not until 1998 that she found her true calling in art. Since then, she has traveled the world as an art instructor and explored her own creative possibilities in drawing and painting. Kate has exhibited in various galleries within BC and Indonesia.

Kate strives for simplicity through her drawings, and then likes to apply bold colors to express a strong sense of style. Her new love is to PLAY with different media to create layers and textures within each painting. She allows these elements to take her in new directions. It gives the art more depth and interest, always with the attempt to be pleasing to the eye.

'I do not work in a formulaic manner, rather I draw and paint, add different media or maybe scrape away areas and then draw and paint some more and continue this PLAYFUL and 'WHAT IF' process until I feel I've achieved a painting that is balanced and pleasing. It is always a creative adventure, and I love it.'

Facing page, clockwise from top left:
Bella Passione – 2013 – mixed media on cradle board
Magenta Peony – 2011 – ink on paper
Sketchbook Collage – 2014 – ink and paper
Blue Birds – 2011 – mixed media on cradle board
Colours of Burma – 2013 – mixed media on cradle board
Ancient Pagodas of Burma – 2013 – mixed media on cradle board
Blue Bottles – 2010 – mixed media on cradle board

Left
Bayside – 2013 – mixed media on cradle board

Right
Ink Series – 2011 – ink on paper

Printed by Island Blue / Printorium Bookworks in Victoria, BC, Canada.
All materials used in printing this book were certified by the Forest Stewardship
Council to meet FSC's strict environmental and social standards.